Night Calling

Judy Gahagan

Night Calling

ENITHARMON PRESS

First published in 2003
by the Enitharmon Press
26B Caversham Road
London NW5 2DU

www.enitharmon.co.uk

Distributed in the UK by
Central Books
99 Wallis Road
London E9 5LN

Distributed in the USA and Canada
by Dufour Editions Inc.
PO Box 7, Chester Springs
PA 19425, USA

ISBN 1 900564 33 5

Enitharmon Press gratefully acknowledges the
financial support of Arts Council England

British Library Cataloguing-in-Publication Data.
A catalogue record for this book is available
from the British Library

Typeset in Bembo by Servis Filmsetting Ltd
and printed in England by
Antony Rowe Ltd

CONTENTS

ACKNOWLEDGEMENTS

Some of these poems first appeared in the following publications:
Ambit, Poetry London Newsletter, PN Review, Soundings, Stand, Tabla.

'Today Our Main Concern' won first prize in the Peterloo Competition 2000; 'May You Have Soft Landings' won first prize in the Canterbury Festival Poetry Competition 1996; 'Rooftop Protest' won third prize in The London Writer's Competition 1994; 'On the Occasion of the First Russian Quiz Show' won fourth prize in the City of Cardiff International Poetry Competition 1994; 'Solstice' won second prize in the Norwich Writer's Circle Open Poetry Competition 2000.

'My Futures Wheel and Fan Like Evening Birds' was selected for the *Forward Book of Poetry 2000*. That poem and 'Tonight' formed part of the sequence *Wellsprings*, poems written by the author for a song cycle, music by Sam Pechter, first performed at the University of York, Spring Festival of New Music 2002.

TO MY PARENTS

*'and the unguarded soul might fly
into the magic circle of the night'*

Hermann Hesse

I think I'd always been waiting for them
waiting for the intensity of their ritual deportment
for the slow beat of their gait, obsequies
of expressionlessness, as they ushered us
(uncouthly alive) into the limousine.
Theirs was the protocol of the deepest bow
the choreography of black silk hats
mimed drama of unutterable humility
as the hearse took precedence, turned, adagio
into the commonplace of traffic.

I knew already that to sit upright behind the dark glass
of the limousine following the hearse
would be a privilege of protocol, and of perspective:
to look out on those too, too familiar streets
of life at its most typical, as if already dead.
Sometimes, on such a day, in the full of life
among people forgetting their shadows
I've looked out, briefly half-alive, invisible
mute and silent behind my own dark glass.

I've waited for their funereal gestures
those acolytes in black to escort us
through the realms of the ceremonial
past the cardboard scenes of the shopping mall
to the dark heart of a solstice, the slow fall
into silence. Don't they promise the abyss
the black velvet rose, the leafless lunar lily
on watch and waiting for us?

We should have chosen protest flowers,
mauve inflorescences of Smoke Bush,
Snowball Tree, Hibiscus, Red Hot Poker,
floral uprisings for the angry dead
in the Garden of Remembrance;

but the brochure offered Rose Bush:
boudoir Floribunda, blousy pinkies,
Princess Mary, Peace or Arlene Francis.

The discretion of our choosing numbed us,
grouped palely under pale, cold birch trees
to choose the Place: escarpment, cromlech,
hero's pike, a bluff, a boulder, some
indignant surge of earth for them,

but the brochure offered Seat
or Niche, Stepping Stone on a winding path to nowhere.
'Peace' and we agreed on the secluded Arbour.

We'd watched his trembling, wafery hand
spoon jelly to his once cantankerous wife
those long last days.
Now we'd leave them
at peace among their neighbours.
Leave them for another country.

For a big country
where the candles burn all night
in walled shrines beyond
the monumental towns,
where the dead glitter their presences
on the great black hills.

THE LIGHTNESS OF NOT BEING

So Emilio was dead.
And I'd brought my winter shoes
sagging from the same old tread
in the same old grooves
for him to mend.

The same old thoughts.

But it's summer now
and his stone kiosk
I'd climb up to is doused
in sun and butterflies;

he'd look up
when my shadow reached
into his cool stone room
to look over my old shoes.

So wafery watery-blue-eyed Emilio
has left his body
for the sea on its bluest days;
today its silk cover's seamed
invisibly and stretched
over faint breathing.

Some people here seem,
like Emilio, like fairy-light bulbs
on a wire hung for a fête,
to flicker and go out in ones
when you're not looking.

They re-appear
as photographs on gravestones
taking death gravely
as Emilio will
in black and white and definite now
though dead

not diaphanous as he was,
eyes filled with the blue after blue
of summer afternoons.

I'm holding out these old shoes
as if to sell them
on some ice-gristled street,
in a terminal grey city.

Isn't this a genetic fault-line
to tread so heavy,
to bring along a shadow to every summer party,
to remember the winter news –
lumpen bodies swilling un-piloted down a river?

But the cumulo-nimbus is climbing
and I remember
how down a different river
they were launching dead souls
in coloured paper lanterns
bobbing with joy
and lightweight as Emilio

to be piloted till the estuarine streams
engulfed them and listing they coalesced
into a collective glimmer
of souls on the edge of the dark.

Emilio's stone room's empty
of his weightless wantless
presence.
The cumulo-nimbus reaches its altitude
and the butterflies dither.

We turned away from the perfect curve
of the cove's white smile
and the candour of days on the beach,
the azures of skies and seas and days too much
to live up to; behind the rocks which ended it
was a kind of antidote: a secret mini-Utah
of furrowed cliffs, great men's profiles
and fossil faces, pitted and blind
where water hauled about by the tides
was toil and regret tugging at the shore;
and just off-shore, by a taciturn rock,
a man, with his back to us and thigh-deep
in the swill, of kelp, of dead men's fingers,
of limey shells, of bloodless molluscs,
beside a small poor ancient boat,
was rummaging in its scuffed cuddy,
winding things and hauling them in, embroiled
in something urgent as if he wanted to hide
from us his mysterious purpose.
A genre scene: 'Fisherman at Low Tide' perhaps
or a ghost, for there was a dark around him.
It shielded us from the bright day –
the unconvincing innocence of the beach;
the white smile, the 'azzurrissimo' (the brochures say)
that's difficult to stay untroubled in –
even for a moment. He retched the engine
into action suddenly then reared up and out,
bumping past a yacht, white logo of pleasure,
to keep his secret, his darkness, intact
far out, dark speck, half-swallowed by the glitter.

SUDDEN HOAR-FROST

This morning I wake petrified: sudden hoar-frost
surrounds my house with wild-haired ancients
frozen alive rampaging where they shouldn't.

The skeins of starved white hair have snagged
streaming from the wards of that Hotel Dieu;
my mother's eyes: 'Why have you brought me here?'

And my hair is deep brown, the unflinching shine
of the ageless conker perpetuating its high noon;
dense mahoganies will outlive me in this room

where most mornings I wake petrified: a presence
assigned in plain clothes, buffs its nails, waiting
for the tactful moment: 'so, as soon as you are ready.'

One day, but not yet, my hair will suddenly go white
overnight, I'll wake to the shock of its hoar-frost
as my mother did, wandering that perilous dawn, lost.

The trees are caught alight, they're burning white fire.
I saw a film once where suddenly enraged and splendidly
an ancient with white hair rode into the sea shouting.

I sense the sift and trickle of gentle replacement
on ceremonial lawns.
At the graduation parties the fathers' shadows are lengthening
to that long moment
the sun's reached, angled low and glowing below the trees.
I'm watching whole families
from the residences of this interchange – where the constant is
replacement, the sift, the trickle –
from the temporary identical thoughtful rooms in blue-grey
patterns of twilit landscapes,
the colours of wisdom, the grey of patience, the blue of
    resignation.
I'm watching parents propped up smiling
in their open-day clothes – as El Cid was strapped into his silver
    armour, dead, stiff arm raised,
and ridden redundant and necessary into a last proud rally.
I watch the sons' and daughters' faces
slant away into the slight breeze, pennants streaming:
'Hi, Lucy, Matt, Pete, hi Cath, Garry, see you later,' to each other.
On their Attic plain of unfenced future.

THE TREES BELIEVE THEY'RE DYING

I'd never thought a summer
could be closing quite so early; this one's drought
has parched its ducts and veins.

The trees believe they're dying,
they exude such a fever of berries;
and a local ancient Quixote

crazy with terminal joy
has draped himself in delirious paper flowers
and strides by singing and shouting

as if he and the trees
must put on this desperate show of fruiting just to plead
another chance.

This is my birthday I walk through
like a ghost prowling among abandoned stalls piled high
with left-overs.

It's been a long time
becoming empty, transparent, invisible, becoming dry-eyed,
drought-stricken

yet I must have walked here once
through days I poured my heart into, days brimming over
with heart-felt rain,

brimming with the tumult
of beginnings and the day-after-day great bowls of summer
I don't remember . . .

I don't remember other birthdays;
dust shrouds the plaster figures of my life
in museum drapes.

This day's mood festoons
the harmless hedges with the purple of deadly nightshade.
And the dark I walk towards

I'd like to greet
as he is: masked and glittering in fantastic costume
before its door.

Tonight I was thinking about death,
just idly, just a furtive touch about it,
watching the darkening hills;

the abysses between them spoke
of the dark clefts in life, only half-attended to.
The evening was sombre

till he arrived with his clamour of life
eyes on full-beam, in a loud jacket,
exploding the twilight.

A golden mist was intensifying beyond the ridge
halo-ing the garden tree:
'The moon,' I ventured, unnecessarily.

He paused for the pinkish-golden fruit
to rise to that perfection
he believed he'd ordered up

then pointed with his steak-knife
at Perseus, Cassiopeia, the Pleiades
and other once enigmatic constellations.

RETURNING TO RUSSIA

The winter here is very long, or hugely slow;
the broken pavements with their gristles of ice last
for a tonnage of unwanted future to be unloaded;

they say that at zero temperature the particles
are absolutely still, no force, no protest;
only the black trees pose, chaotic and hysterical

to mime the violence iced-in behind
the pale fuse of dusk; its light is the light
and lingering glance of long green eyes.

I've returned to this place like the seagull
returns, to where things lie spookily about,
returned from afternoons of racing-blue
and funny hats, carousing with the new jokes
of the year, the tiny photogenic moments.
I've returned to the grey communal bread,
to a place inside myself I can't forget.

Muffled children poke the ice with sticks
incurious, in silence, not breaking it.
And another endless night lowers itself.

FUNFAIR NEAR CHERNOBYL

Ah, desolation comes on in such frail colours:
a glitch in the inner voltage, a dipping of the mood
when I come upon a photo of a dead funfair

by Chernobyl, of dodgems draped in rotted shrouds;
so the gold of birch leaves outside the kitchen
turns now, as if the sun went in, to yellowish;

as if it tried to shine across those defunct marshlands
where the grasses rust, the town's abandoned,
the plant imploded. Ah, just the funfair's enough

for the delicacy of desolation. It hovers frail
over the loneliness of landscapes once fabulous –
in this here too crude and bright for it now.

Some time to come in the longest memories
of the oldest there'll be no trace of vibrant worlds
that were bright gold. They'll think it's always been like this.

A Long-Drawn-Out Coronation

These mornings I wake to the long-drawn-out
coronation of the trees in a thinning garden;
so slow it is and the garden contradictory;

the light sheers off the last of the leaves leaving
decrepitude, pools of light just opulent where the sun
gold-leaves the arras, pours coins into the garden's bowl.

Was I ever present at the coronation of my own happiness?
No, I never made that techni-colour Fall
in a big country, the gala nights and sunset boulevards.

This last home run is slow, is contradictory.
Last night, after what seemed an infinity of darkness
still hours to go till midnight, as if there were war

or someone in mourning to be watched over, I saw
suddenly beyond the black panes of emptiness
the birch tree, incandescent copper against the night.

But no crowning moment, always contradictory.
One tree holds out black seed-bags, its burdens
of grief beyond reason even before the light begins to fade

while the other gathers in the gold, reaches back
into summertime triumphs and gala nights, glows on
as if it would cease to breathe still wearing its tiaras.

FIELD FOR THE LOW SEASON

Between the shunted-off stub of the old road
and the new one – Aurelia, plundering its way South

over fields of sunflowers, unanimous,
their blaze being the simple colour of success –

lie the remains of a field,
refuge to an underclass of haphazard sunflowers

hanging around,
as I am too, walking here where no one walks.

Their eyes button-hole me
into the conviviality of derelicts.

They have only each other
and this field without a name or purpose

to be frail and disorderly in.

This field is for the low seasons
and the twilit subtle hues of failure.

But I know that a month or so on
when precision-planting has become

scorched earth, a mass black death,
(festivities should not have planned ends),

here in seed-packed entropy, among whisps and drabs,
death will be quiet, gradual, uncertain.

SOLSTICE

This is the season of short to vanishing days,
for retreats into interiors within interiors
into the centre of the season's candlelight.
Shapes in long black inhabit the dusk.
But there are some who flee the solstice, search out
some other season's bright hard surface.

It's symbiotic here below the surface,
our roots snarled up. The short grey days
feel curfewed, furtive we slip out
and back into curtained-off interiors,
into their carved gilt frames. Dusk
mingles with snow, snuffing out the light.

And yet this is a festival of light:
where joy is deep, glittering bubbles to the surface
wantonly – the feasts and fanfares start at dusk.
The others resist this underworld, their days
are safari-treks away from dark interiors
to the loose-limbed beaches, the sunlit out

of doors, the light blue freedom, out
in a heroic world of action, fun-packed, light-
weight, soul-free. Their interiors
are minimalist, the cool hard surface
of the dispassionate life measures out the days,
aligning them to stave off perilous dusk.

For the realities they construct melt down at dusk,
the high-noon versions peter out.
We, incurious, shelter in short dark days
in the warmth of darkness lit by candle-light.
Even the deepest shadows have no surface
where solstice reveals the rich interiors.

The hinterlands are mystery. Our interiors,
locked cabinets, are unlocked at dusk.
Velvet hearses glide beneath the surface
as we blow the fragrant candles out
and the winter night reigns unchallenged. Light
from its speechless planets dwarfs the days.

And light glows deepest on the darkest days.
Dusk, an evanescent surface, shrouds
the way out, cocoons the honeycombed interiors.

WATCHING THE SWIFTS

I longed for some end to perpetual flight
the sheer verve of risk ventures
sudden dives to the pits
they feed on the nothings which themselves live on air.

I dreaded whole cities where there's no private life
ritzy interiors rebuff any intimacy
opaque-eyed dealers ponder their futures
the diaphonous futures conjured out of the air.

I wanted to feel that as dusk gentled the light
they'd get more personal, the swifts,
touch on things more completely
creep under the roof-tiles to reflect in the dark.

But black bounces still ditto among the old chimneys
on sky-high parabolas swept up from the depths
they shriek and assault the weakening air
they are bored with the twilight, allergic to gentling.

There's nowhere to go. No escape from fast turn-over
from the sell-outs and free-falls
the one-fell-swoop take-overs
which make all that is solid melt into air.

I should get out of here
breast-stroke it, crawl or claw my way out
of the encircling lagoon;
find the channels where the ocean-going liners
slip without fuss
into the open sea and the boisterous sparkle.

Don't look now
or you'll turn back to the life of the labyrinth
further and deeper in.
The black gondola is shaped for paranoia
threading its needle
through the backwaters of the unconscious.

And it has an edge –
the toothed blade of the *ferro*, a weapon
a spiteful swan would aim.
The gondola is the cradle and the coffin
so don't relax
into its damask cushion, don't admire its golden rose,

it's trying it on with its song
for those plumped up, half at ease and smiling
at the old black magic;
'O, *sole mio*' they sing to clients in winter *loden* coats.
But this is moon territory
not sun and the sparkling health salts of the open sea.

in a crimson pearl-hung Boyar's cloak
polite inside a hook-nose jeering half-moon head
masked and crawling in yellow bombazine

me smoking a hookah in a preposterous turban?
My Self, small chrysalis, in a frilly heap of satin
trampled and snuffed in a pageant of transvestites.

She'd said half-joking: 'I want to go
as one of the Three Graces.' She so wan, so thin
flailing around in peachy crêpe de Chine

for Venice was arctic. Snow had laid its white fur rim
on the black gondolas; the lagoon lay ice-locked
the sails of Cleopatra's barge were frozen taut.

When a troupe of gold-faced clones, inscrutable
in ruby moiré outsized ball-gowns ringed us
bowing and scraping in a frisson of fans, mocked us:

'True self? There's nothing but Appearances!'

the carnival drums shattered the canal's black glass
music filtered through black alleys, courtyards, ghettos
filling the chambers of that city, onion without a heart

filling the cavities where a Self might just have lurked.

LETTING GO IN VENICE

I slip this winter night
down the *Canale Grande* of a life
of palaces, empty
behind their traceries of arches,
column clusters, quatrefoil . . . my Coat of Arms,
the pronouncements I'd hoped
to be admired for, not loved,
not real they gaze into their wavering reflections.

What is terra firma
but the *fondamente* of attitudes, positions
taken up? I light up
now with douce pink lamps
their mausoleum.
The last lights tonight
will be the chandelier in the *piano nobile,*
the guardian light at my water-gate.

Black water barcarolles
what light there's left
to fold it into its bales of silk
into black backwaters;
lights the iron grills sunk in the slime
on which everything is built –
sunk in untenable basements.

What's left tonight
of attitudes, positions? My hawkish edicts stand upright
on deck beneath the crimson canopy
of the *bucintoro.*
I caress the old head
of some poetic phrase I was about to utter:
it rises to speak in its Doge's hat,
pale, and drained of all authority.

'What's Beauty then, old bonehead?'
I think he's dead. I hear stilled wind,
we're entering the lagoon,
it's pewtered for the winter.
Somehow I missed the masked ball, the regatta,
the cheap and pungent sparkle
of the open summer sea.

EXORCIST

I lugged home
half my weight in pumpkins
to line up on the kitchen table

each bland head
to be trepanned, de-pulped,
the flesh gouged out
for the fiery calabash
only I would eat

then got down to work

to make them two-faced:
each would have a Hyde
to his Jekyll,
one side a yokel's grin
till a sudden swivel
in the wind
and he'd face them
with his ghastly self.

I lined up my nightlights,
waxy little souls
in clean paper jackets,
lowered them in clear of the string
and carried my lamps
into the darkening garden
to hang from gibbets
to be stuck on spikes.

Around midnight I toured the baby Hades
of a suburban garden.

Their schizoid selves
had vanished:
they'd softened into disembodied
smiles of light
glowing all around
seraphic little Buddhas.

ROOFTOP PROTEST

It's most likely to be in spring
the prisoners break out

and head for the roof
in joke-burglar clothes
with looted megaphones
to caper in space –

the space, the space
the Himalayan spaces of it –

and look down on treeless yards
where alleys are blind
maze after cruciform maze

no one ever learns
and shout: 'We're human!'

And breathe the air –
the air, the air
great fizzy gulps of it!

It's mostly in spring
when better weather makes
rooftop protest more attractive
prisoners break out onto the roof

to scan shapeless horizons
for signs of mountains
glints of water, roads
to once imagined places

scan the grid-locks
beyond the treeless yards
for the un-convicted.

SAVING THE PITS

Perched on a thin cortex of suburban turf uneasy,
up there the stars so far away and freezing, we needed
chthonic black and slow millennial combustion

but feared the other pits – depression turning into slump,
the chronic lethargy of low-turnover, lost in shadows,
messes, repressed ghettos miles below the shining.

We needed miners. Hewing at the heart of things down there,
lit up all night, mechanised as modern gynaecology,
at home down there at the bottom where sludge can turn to gold.

That day they burst up black-faced, white-eyed, collective, good,
so we followed them like children to a faraway with banners
to save ourselves from the starvation of no underworld.

That day the rain dripped on the fat lips of the tubas,
someone shouted: '*stop raining!*' But it could not.
Rain is the love that joins up earth with heaven.*

The miners blazed and thundered at the wedding
and we were united too for this moment:
the return of the umbrae, our very heroes from the underworld.

But knew at heart and dreaded the huge bones
of advanced technology rotting in sealed tombs
roofs caving in, water filling, Hades at large and roaming.

* *It rained all day on the march for the miners in 1984*

'MAY YOU HAVE SOFT LANDINGS'

(a toast once popular with aeroflot pilots)

I would fly with them
through the latitudes and longitudes of crash statistics;
with veteran fighter pilots young again, artistes,
who love to fly their magic machines
high, high above the thievery of the markets;

and I would drink with them
the pure spirit, the clandestine clink-less toast
to the unspeakable beauty of the world
while their eyes slit with mirth
as the risks get more piquant:
'May you fly till your soul sings above the clouds!'
'May you have soft landings!'

The hostesses are getting prettier –
slippery green eyes, unfettered curls.
They slide laughing down the practice chute
shrieking for another go.
And I would go and laugh with them:
'May you land softly in the arms of birch woods!'
'May you parachute like twilit snowflakes falling!'

Those pilots who keep their bear-hug bodies strong
in the steam house with the birch whip,
juniper thrash, with vodka more vodka,
I would fly with them
and practise the toast without a clink
as the risks get more piquant:
'To quantum fields, to virtual mechanics, to soft landings!'

Once this veteran brought down
to earth his plane-load of Holy sleepers:
no instruments, no lights, no visibility
anywhere in the universe;
his faith in God and vodka
was huge and dark.
And it was a soft landing!

Seeing that the people seemed to love
the toothy compère, spontaneous applause,
the absolutely infinitesimal chance
of winning the dream-car on its plinth
in this fairest of innocent games,
they've ordered up a wintry travesty of this,
the TV Quiz Show, before a non-invited audience;
someone known for his interrogations constructs
some leading questions concerning the infinity
of random facts extant in the universe
for glacial prizes from a crystal chaos of cut glass
decanters, the last tear-drops of looted chandeliers.

The girl is a Snow Queen in silver boots,
an ice-chip in her heart, her laser eye
selects the victims with a tinsel wand
while in the spirit of democracy
the camera pans without mercy the floor
of sprawling dishevelled players:
a Dr Caligari box of madmen beyond desire,
despair, guarded by a mystic black-wigged spy.

Someone's actually won! A crystal cake-stand
with no cake! The band goes mad! She waves her wand!
The audience disintegrates as the camera tracks
the winner's uncertain path out to dark slush
to goose-step round an Eternal Flame;
while our boys and girls are creamily content
with the fair questions and winning everything or
nothing. The tail-lights of their real cars wink
into that darkness where there are no prizes at all
and un-watched the eternal flame's gone out.

GREEN LANES WITH SKATEBOARDER

The skyline was moody and rough
everyone heading off towards
their various disappointments
up Green Lanes in small dull bursts

when down Green Lanes a single figure
gliding through the broken straggle
appeared: seraphic, mobile,
an unlikely Visitation

from the lemony morning sky
flowing past the station beggars
on a secret current, crossing
the slight river's own contra-flow

till at ten yards off it took shape
as a Chinese boy on a skateboard
smiling to his Walkman, removed
from the clog and thwart of traffic.

His drift was smooth, swift as a gull's
whose single wing flick missed you gazed
rapt at its infinite cadence
his face unmarked as the fading moon.

As If it Were a Present to Us

From rows of windows we see them
skinning alive the deep green field
to make a car-park.

The top-soil the grab is lifting high
and pouring is a fine and gentle rain
onto the two toy lorries

and they kept busy through the gloaming
of a long slow winter afternoon, the trees,
old mutes, looking on

the men, also toy men, wooden men,
and husband-men, and in their yellow helmets
trusted to see this job through

as if it were a present to us, the car-park,
we'll look at from the rows of windows,
from the square places:

Emergency Exits, Dry Riser Outlets, Stores.
The hearts in these laboratories are ready
to be by-passed, wind-dried

sifted through dispassionately
while trees unclothed and innocent as Jesus try to shroud
the frightened semi-de-s

from the bloodbath of a winter sunset.

in a low-lying landscape.
A flat dead sea
of small ordinary houses
laps the precinct
of portakabins
inscrutable chimneys

but from Business Studies come
three black princesses, gold hung,
and a Genghis Khan strides by in a scarlet shirt –
such dark, dark eyes, such freedom smiles.

Access paths lead
from one function
to another function;
stick-men behind theodolites
spy out the land
in micro-angles

till beyond new developments it absconds
under a widening sky, lemony, hopeful
and seawards, seawards.

The Directors' Car-park
box-hedged and flowerless
nothing to challenge
the pillared awe
of the Main Entrance
except four yew trees

but suddenly a slow bell strikes the hour
as if this Hour now were an Office watched over by an angel

Around dusk I'd just crept out and startled
saw the full moon peering through a blizzard
so low, like a stricken jet, it barely cleared
the tail-back to the petrol station, the exhausted
school the kids had sacked; right now they surged
round the Kentucky with huge mouths, unspent
force and the moon kept peering as best it could,
as we all must, trepidatious, through the ferment.
But then I thought, and here I interrupt the argument
to contemplate the winter: how the winter might
bring a slowing of the heart, the breath, a slackening
of the will; and in its long go-slow, a taking-stock
of the galore of centuries, of techno-products waiting
in vast showrooms like unsold chandeliers, so the shock
of the new could wait. By now the moon was swimming
high above the cluttering pylons, high above the tail-back.

The Lake Belongs to the University

I

The gnats are dancing
just beyond the reach of privileged footsteps.

The lake belongs to the university
a concrete ship
beached and stranded
on glowing clovery high ground.

By the artificial lake
the real dawn mists would rise
in silence

but for the incessant knowing hum
of the university's thoughts
the billion ideas
simmering in its concrete brain.

The lake has a simple life:
mostly flowing northwards fast
till the breeze tilts
turns it around and suddenly
it flows fast south;

the dumb wisecracks of water birds
their amazing V-shaped glimmers
the skitter of one took off
airlifting its hapless legs into the sunset

this seems enough for hours.

II

Long ago they thought
the university would need a lake
now the scholars mostly jog
twice round crashing the paths
wall-eyed with purpose

and on Saturday nights
the university shut down
the lake withdrawn into itself,
on concrete walkways, plazas, steps,
the T-shirt logos bellow
Hell, Anthrax, Balls.

III

It is autumn it is raining
the university is sick
its concrete has cancer
and is turning black.
The bilges pour down heavy water
onto thin flat roofs
above the sleepers.

The lake churns its mud up in sympathy.

IV

But now in spring
from the inert heart
of a high-up classroom I look out:

the lake has come out of its woodlands
it stretches wide and extroverted
as America, its sparkles are dancing
suddenly in a sudden sun-burst

bringing unlimited supplies of joy
to the university
which in itself
is neither joyful nor melancholy
but objective
its concrete reflects nothing
but an earnest wish
to excavate the truth

as once they dug the lake out.

Only there is another truth
a peaceful one:

in the secret reaches
each tall willow has one huge branch split
from reaching down
in thirst, in longing
for the water's black sleep.

SHORT LEAVE

The tight knit of life would unwind
itself to a single thread: the road north-west
spooling onto the lure of cobalt hills
one way, as if we'd never need return.

At the two-thirds mark a ruthless stretch:
three lanes – high above a no-man's land
the only turn-off to coils of road to nowhere
we could bear to go to – reduced to one; here

we'd see the choir of cooling towers keeping abreast
as we veered pure west persisting on the horizon
as if they couldn't bear to let us go. Each one
breathed out a slow aaah of exhausted breath

seeming to sing like heavy sirens: '*don't go on –
you belong to us*', not to neolithic outcrops
awash in auburn seas of bracken, to remaindered wilds
where you'll find no home, '*there is no other home*'

where you'll stare through mist at cromlechs
sheep gawping from black slits in brimstone eyes.
'*You come too late, to be children of the hills*'
but the road lured us, as it always had, on

as the choir of cooling towers fell back, the sun
subsided still flushed behind the cobalt hills
now crowning the horizon, hills that would surround us
like friends in the morning for our short leave.

Where the climb and the gale stifle the debate
where the beeches face the sea defenceless
all's reduced to the splendour of great height
the last quivering leaves, like us, breathless
from the big argument. Only iron
branches elbow out on this side, the sea side,
the gale side, trunks blasted to a sheen
gun-grey, so absolute we disregard

the lapse and flux of colours too fleeting
to fix with names – green swilling over amber –
and the fields below unstable. The beeches
could recall copperiness or rustling
sweet attics diverting us all the summer
and somehow confusing clear-cut issues.

FIELD FOR RETURNING HOME

And I'd have made my home in a small corner
of this vast field frontiered by the forest –
a field too vast too strong to be a summer meadow

so vast three mini-humans on millimetre bikes
have barely moved one notch across its brow
their scant headway makes me small too

powerless, happy to be absorbed in the field's vast
scheme of things and on the threshold of the winter;

today a last disorderly silk unfurls across the sky
the plough knits dun plain to a rich dark purl
the strips of thin green shoots are drizzling away
to an horizon fainting with distance –

and I'd have cycled hunched through dark mornings
to low-key work along the railway track
past the liquorice chimney, wood-yard, gravel pit,
the forest breathing out its warm sighs, and back
home, eye-level with huge clods, the winter green,
the field drawing in the last of the light.

Today I would have talked about amygdala,
almond-shaped clusters of inter-connected structures
perched above the brain stem –

but today was ominous:
inner and outer weather mingled around the campus
in a tide of cobalt clouds.

Amygdala, little almond,
I would have told them it was you who runs these loops
of low-grade melodrama –

but a gull was crying
above the concrete temple of the Arts Block
as if it had forgotten the sea.

I would have taken them through the limbic system
and the ancestral environments of our feelings,
explained the neural hi-jackings

but feared I might be mad myself,
sing turmoil at them,
sing the syrupy vernacular of the heart

and they'd be waiting
faceless, rising tier on tier like placid saints,
the dispassionate white screen waiting

to be scrawled with the graffiti of frets and angst,
the PA system sense the drowning hollows
of my voice and boom uncertainty.

Today our main concern . . . our main concern will be
the cohorts of our intimate enemies,
the toxic thoughts, the case of love . . .

KEEPING THE WATER MOVING

Though I knew
it was better not to speak of tears or any other kind of water
as a metaphor for tears,

knew better than to stand
watching the rain's plummeting down of daylong grief, its pour
dissolving the heroic profiles of the mountains,

still I watched it and feared
how the geometry of the ditches it had taken a century of
   self-discipline
to precision-cut the plain with

would be obliterated,
the plain relapse to the shore-less miasmic swamp it once was,
feared being sucked down

beneath the floating peats
falling into hidden wells.
I fear the bogs of feeling, feeling, feeling.

Though I remembered
how the rivers from the mountains flush
all matter of no consequence

in their rush to get away,
how the rinsed light of tomorrow's morning will re-trace
the precise mica of the ditches

shine the purpose of the roads,

yet still I looked
and the raindrops trapped in the mosquito mesh of this small
   window
looked to me like tears

and the mesh a limen
held between the outer order of tough perspective, controlled
   irrigation
to keep the water moving

and an inner one, low delta, sapped
but teeming with truths lived below the surfaces that give
   themselves away
in leaks of sweats and tears.

Clematis petals follow me in –
winged seeds, pollen and various dusts –
when I close the door for the night
on the copious garden;
                behind me the house is inert,
the air unstirred, the surfaces untouched.
The house can't be inhabited enough
                for that lived-in look
the garden doesn't need.

I close the door reluctantly
on the massing dark of the trees.
They open their arms
to welcome me into a night in the forest,
to sleep amidst its intense activities.

It was another kind of life
in the rare air of glass high-rises
beyond the reach of roving seeds, stray flies,
the darkness never quite arriving –
the life I couldn't lead.

This time, this hour,
this doorway is a cusp
where even now I don't quite dwell.
The seasons should dissolve
into one another as the sift of May
drifts in. But they collide here.
May is erupting
into the autumn of the house –
the hermitage of its rooms –
dark curtains, the peace of long winter.

Permit River

There is a secret river and a silent river
beyond the fencing of the micro-wilderness
by the railway, a local river, a man-made river;
but still it swathes itself over wide-eyed stones
swiftly fingering the grass curtains hung from the banks.
Ducks gather and the local park's two swans
inspect, unhurriedly, this reach, then deign
to fall in love with themselves in the brown, bright mirror.

It's not the river I always wanted –
a mountain river pouring through the sleep
of a narrow, shuttered town in its incessant rush
to reach somewhere mythical. It's not
the dark highway where lighter boats advance
great ships to the ports that greet them
with songs in many languages. This river
is a little bonus like the wilderness. But fretted over

when, in summer, they shut the filter beds
somewhere further down, nearer to the city
and we come upon a river that is motionless
and silting up and the slime closing in.
The ducks give up at the soft advance of the rheum
where cans vegetate. It's part of some plan
to regulate the flow, but it's not the river's own –
longing to join another river or even reach the sea.

Then we give up on it for weeks till suddenly
pushing through the permitted micro-wilderness
there's a sense of cool, of current, of the silence
a silent river airs. They've opened up the filter beds
again, somewhere further down and nearer to the city,
so it finds again its undertow, reveals its depths
and the swans are back to inspect those secret reaches
below the road bridge where it (briefly) disappears.

53

BABUSHKA

Just standing smiling like a painted doll,
babushka, standing among the minders,
the children who climb and stare. This park's a kraal
for women who just stand there while the day simmers
slowly and water birds take off in shimmers
and squawks. For me, for the child's child I mind,
littlest of the nested dolls I dither around,
having to, even wanting to, but once I pined
for flight, for great leaps forward, not resigned . . .

'There, that's better' . . . his cheerful baby's face
blossoms now from inside his woolly hat
with earflaps, inside his quilted space suit,
deep in a fleecy pram. This habitat
is winter. Swaddling and smothering compete
to keep warm the old alibis (and him)
for dropping out of the thrust and cut
and ice of life out there. Old babushka, I'm
universal, invisible, but forever smiling.

His bright rooms of sing-song voices
replace the dreams I dreamed of being visible . . .
of being, loud, unique! They dwindle smiling, voiceless
vanishing dolls, each trapped inside another doll.
Babushka, little mother, you'd never spoil
this peace with regret. You'd smile at the swan
as he is smiling and crowing at the gull's
pyrotechnic cut and thrust, cold freedom –
his future, my lost past. This is our oblivion

this the quietude of Russian peasants
laying in potatoes in Holy rows
beneath the house, babushkas, self-sufficient,
swaddled in skirts, shovelling snow, squash-nosed,
disregarded, but eternal. If I chose
to be a smiling patient person it was fear
of a worse oblivion: the big slack shadows
of failure, obsolescence, drove me here
to squat in a humble place, nested, near-and-dear.

I don't know what he sees, I see his smiles
when a sudden rush of light floods the trees
the silver flickers from the under-wings of gulls
figure-skating above the lake. His smiles appease
the shame of having given in – the ease of it
was pitiful, abject. And yet that alibi
was more than an alibi, it was a grasp on, a lease
on that love without agenda we, half mute, cry
out for. Babushka, little mother, so do I!

I do and yet I know I must move on,
the clouds move on, birds circle and wheel
and in me too a youth, like a thin man
inside a fat man (nested like a doll)
struggles to get out, to ignore the roll call
to generation without end, to wheel and soar
in the thin pure air where time is still,
the solitude absolute – I must endure that
too – but not yet. I stand here, rooted, still unsure. . .

EXILES: PEARL RIVER DELTA

You and I have lost our roots.
You – pocky, half-caste fruit –
have forgotten your citrus groves
by the forest's clambering halls of flowers
under the incessant drum and pour
of the monsoon on huge leaves.

And I wilt – old, crumpled, waiting
for the heavy afternoon to melt
into the blurred lights that move
only where the Pearl River moves,
inside the open jaws of China –
marooned on a global tide of concrete

too high up to hear again the green din
of our first garden here, too old to revive
the earth chill in the orchards, the roots
I left too many oceanic nights on board ago;
nights dancing with the officers; the green
fizz of those lychee trees the green of that dress . . .

but I remember the strange hush
of small servants in paper mules
bringing the fruit in lacquered bowls
and laying out the shantung coats
for my morning rides; tedious nights
of yet another rubber while the moon hung

above the harbour. Today the fruit is sullen:
bananas ganged up like indentured labour
that could turn nasty; and she *will* bring durian,
the girl, delicious pulp, appalling stench,
I've *told* her not to. Today I've no appetite
for anything but gazing out into the dilating light

once the rain's let up to the unchanged mountains
far beyond Pearl River and its business, beyond
the century and the worst of it, the dulled
purposes of the harbour, the dulling purposes
of titanic China, to those mountains
beyond these orchards, scheduled to be torn down.

Walking the marsh-edged interminable miles
of shore, the hills beyond the estuary far
as when we set out, at loggerheads

and looking at nothing, or nothing but white sails
far out on the empty shining, in fours,
eights, quadrilles, turning, retreating, a nautical

come-dancing and we walking into an impasse
of distance, smallness, futility, futile talk
that is, and my eye roving to escape this isthmus

to follow them, white, free, leading off
in consensual two by twos, to disappear.

It's this breach keeps us together,
poles apart, our versions antipodean.
Mine's clear, plain, white. I see no other.

And so we keep on walking on the spot
and nothing brings the empty shining future
any nearer, nor us to lightness, to shift.

Other sails are flitting back now, motley,
tacking and turning their orange, pink, green,
blue on blue, each *paso doble* a mirage,

for now they're changed by some sleight
beyond the horizon, they've taken on a camouflage
of colours, to advance, reciprocate, pass, re-pass.

How come we can't? Find a space to be
sea-changed, protean, disparate, together
for the *paso doble*?

And suddenly I can see clearly:
the same sails, white on one side
coloured on the other: one sail two sides

dancing their vis-à-vis, their both, their either way
as the sea's reversing its blues and greens, its bands
of pearl and opal close to the horizon.

Nothing is forever.
The hills beyond the estuary have moved up,
for distances collapse when storms loom and weather

casts its slant on things; this walk, this talk
will founder. Turning I see the inland greens imploding,
turning again that the sails have vanished.

The fact is – the grandeur of the vision
is best preserved
where the living are a small minority

like here; and here they're only fitful
vanishing down the lugubrious alleys
of crowding trees or stooped over heaps of clay.

Today we've brought Cyclamen and Hebe
to my father, buried here among old heroes;
his mantelpiece orations too had grandeur

though, like theirs, they're lost on the wind.
Today the people come in dribs and drabs
young and mostly dark and always serious

to bring unseasonable carnations, a single rose
to that vast living mind impaled
upon a limb-less concrete plinth

at the confluence of two broad paths
one leading to my father, past
all the other heroes of all the other struggles,

the other through the angels
and ivy-wreaths, the perfumed sentiments
that are lost but not replaced.

Outside this cemetery the world is boastful
having been there, seen it, done it.
It's in here the flitting's nebulous,

this flying day, as fluff,
as the winged seed-clocks drifting like souls
in sudden flocks around the graves.

AS PESSOA SAYS

there's nowhere you can be
without yourself
without your irritating presence
interposed

between an impulse
and the lively scenes
of life beyond –
where you are not.

And Pessoa would ask

if you believed
the soul-subduing indigo
of unattainable hills,
shouldering the burden
of incandescent sunsets
night after night,
the small villages, bored by day,
at night become
miniature Manhattans
of promise,
where you are not

would lay to rest
your endless plans
to be some place else,
where you are not.

Pessoa's own interminable evening

the weary, mauvish
just-before-or-after-rain of Lisbon skies,
no inflation sought,
no cheap hopes

like this search of mine
for the place, perfect because
I am not, was not, will not
be there ever –

large voyeur, conspicuous tourist.

And Pessoa said since you can't escape you

best stay here, do nothing,
don't do today what can be left
for tomorrow, and if possible
not then either.

TO THE AIRPORT

The airport's the last station on the longest line
to the unnamed, unknown sprawling, to the zone
where no one goes, except to the airport, to its shining;

and the passengers get out in little groups beneath pure
white steel fan-tracery that vaults the halls of sheer
glass, hung with crystal mobiles turning and turning –

a conspiracy of silence as if this were the gate to heaven.
Three hostesses point the way to the long haul destinations
smiling, wimpled in turquoise, pink, in almond green.

There's no baggage, shopping, bars, but split-timed care
for the innocent passengers; only the journey matters here.
But first they must pass to the barriers for all Departures

where clutched, extended families weep; even the men,
the new-born just arrived, even the oldest, nearly gone
beyond the general rage to live, are weeping openly.

Escorted through hush to carpeted lift the grey doors
slide to gulp them. Before the brief dark they pause
to wave and go down . . . To fly up through time zones

amnesiac among strangers, into a radiant morning
the other side of the world, another quotidian formed in
time-shifts missing cataclysms by seconds or aeons.

Above this red-ringed day, this interruption, this abyss,
the routine flight paths thread the clouds to a blissed-
out place on the Destinations board, to pre-recorded gongs . . .

'*The making of lace by hand is a metaphor for living*' –
I heard and liked it. The intricacy made of holes
is so flawless I had to see the making of it
watch them shift the pins to follow the cordonnet
purl frail bridges across the emptinesses
to reach illusory islands of leaf sprays
watch them appliqué the mirage to the reticule.

Nun's work and the practising of patience
tatting one square of emptiness a month
an intricate fragment of an unseen whole
some girl with an actual life would veil
herself in intrigue in, singing all the while
the *chansons à toilé*, their walled life
a hunched eternity till the lace is achieved
and leaves its cushion, the discarded underpinning –
and lo, the flawless fiction of someone else's life!

But the long road to the lace school led away
from the pretty-pretty centre of that town
where water-light flickered on ancient stone
pleased trees regarded themselves in mirrored sky
to a low zone, scrubbed and punitively clean.
At the end of that road was the lace school.

We pushed through the door of the surly house
heard first the clack-clack of the bobbins
then saw their big hands hurling them about:
sixteen working women, guffawing not singing,
telling life straight – first this, then that;
and a slow boy with a bashful face, a beginner
perusing the cordonnet in the din.
His ears reddened as I watched and thought:
this is no better than the slash-and-burn of my life
gapings cobbled somehow, loose ends orphaned
the whole awry as you are when you've lost
the raw materials, threads, stuffs, pins,
the pattern inscrutable in the confusion.

Yet still I went on watching hard their hands
for an embryo of order to emerge from the tangle
but saw none – no rosebud, leaf-spray, no *punto in aria*.
Yet, in the chilly showroom, the finished products:
Pristine d'Oyleys, collars, camisoles, runners, cuffs,
the snowdrifts of shawls, draped on the walls.

And between them carved in letters white on ecru
this motto thickly accusing everyone which read:
'*he who has no taste for our daily bread
will never taste the bread of Eternal Life . . .*'
I thought: after the duplicities of this life wait
the hard-spun truths of that unmarked white desert.

SKIERS

Today the falling light
was shining through drops hung on lower branches
hung not just with diamonds

with peridot, amethyst, ruby, lapis
this jewel-house was quite enough to watch –
but there were lone skiers in the distance

winging their Odyssean way
a peculiar up-swinging fast walk
across the whites, the greys

threading the fragile mists on the meadows
mists that leave the church stranded
its golden onion-dome shining

like a lighthouse; lonely
balletic pilgrims skirting the shadows of the forest
the stilled grey trees filmed with valley mist

the bunting of ski-dancers
re-emerging onto diamond-studded flats
along the river seeming to hear

the trickle of water-voices, the half-frozen song.

Close up they'd face you with purpose
their faces shuttered, eyeless
achieving the speed, the distance, the goal.

Far off, unfazed by the vagaries of dusk,
they set out as the sun ignites the last gold flecks
across the snow, streams pink streaks

across the dying sky, pressing on into night;
the scansion of their strange rhythm
counter-points the fusions of sundown.

I'm left with nothing but that movement,
herring-bone weaving through the darkness;
I still move with it behind my eyes.

Picture it then: the lake so still it's trembled
by a falling leaf, the pent-up glory
of the forest trembling, deeply up-turned
in the lake, dark branches hung royally
with scarves of maroon and crimson;
and even shrivelled leaves, in this light
of marigold, buffed wood flowers, glisten.
Picture it but stay silent. You're on a tight
budget for words, for joy, for words of joy
for the great rubescent fugues, the alloys
of old gold. Little is left for you to say
about them in a cold-water regime
whose police mock and expurgate unseen.
It's in golden autumn I seek asylum.

HOUR OF THE WOLF

It's sudden, the waking
at the *hour of the wolf*
small hour, huge solitude.

The triggered beam of a watch-light
on the lawn flushes out the dark
and stops at the white lilac:

its summery clusters move
like plaster casts in unison
in the stirred dark air;

those chalk masks
at *the hour of the wolf*
are a choir of executioners;

the spectral white is the light
of the path the moon's laid down
the garden, for one

as white was the One True Path
the black Watchtower seller
pushed towards me

eyes so swimming with faith
I thought she might be blind
to what I know:

white is the colour of purging.
Above the churning black of the garden
white is the blank of the moon.

I looked out of the window
into moonlit space
where I should have stayed out
let the peace invade
the dark – not just absence of light
but the murk that hangs around
the intransigence of life
with other people;
                              the darkness that brings
body bags for the rubble
left by anger.
                              I could have stayed out
walked abroad diaphanous
through the bridal light, moonlight
as I'd only ever seen it once
in a film – *Les Amants* – with music
they walked or rather glided to.
                              Below, a little path
dun and ordinary by day
was shining white, intense with destination
down the mysterious aisle
the rising trees a guard of honour –

                              I sensed with a silvery calm
that if I'm here or not
the eternal returning of the moonlight
enchants and re-enchants that path
and other forgotten bridal tracts of life
mysterious touched by silver
made ordinary come morning.

And when my far-flung child called up
from the stranger's fastness of her adult life
and we talked through the singing silver air
I saw for a moment a map of the world by night –
the black gape of unpeopled zones, the seething radials
of boom-towns – turning in vast space between us.

It was such a night: the sky's black lid
open to Sirius and other diamonds big as the Ritz
the adamantine stare of the moon at rest;
star-dust rained frost onto summer fields.
'D'you see a huge star . . . like burning coals
in a bucket . . . between the horizon and the moon . . .?'

And thinking at least we saw the same night sky
the same radiance, I felt like singing to it –
and to our great fortune in moon-clichés:
cheap repros of moons hung in stagey trees
ogling themselves in rapt seas, moonlight sonata,
clair de lune, all lovesongs to the silvery moon

even though it drifts, tactless, over death zones
and part of me knows the times a spoiled moon
creeps about a graveyard of sickening clouds
like a vagrant around the city trash-cans;
that to persist in singing to a mute rock hurled
from the vast gasbags of the cosmos is absurd.

And part of me skulks, subversive, waiting
for the radiance to return, for silver to fill
the veins of the night, for permission to sing.
Our wary talk, pulsing through the zinging
silver air, among a billion orphaned kilobytes
was held symbiotic in the fluid of the lovely night.

TONIGHT

Tonight's the night
the sea not even whispering,
keeping its excitement to itself,

it's lifted the pier high
out of the silent swirl of black water

lifted the jokes and bubbling lights,
the theatres of cut-out people,

crystal palaces, roofs so merry with secrets
the pebbles are longing to break into crunch.

And tonight will be the night
in dark parks behind the shore
tree-domes will fill with wordless singing

invisible parties in full swing
on the floating pavilions of Cedars of Lebanon.

The stone lion's eye is heavy with sleep-dust.

Moonlight has frozen the dancing and dancing.

The thousandth night a tonight has been like this.
And a window opens to the cool breath of invitation
framing a never-was-young face

peering through the lace of its wrinkles
for the first night again.

The Day of the Dead
the one big bell is tolling, deep-mouthed
to drown out the small-town
chit-chat with its one tone
its loud opinion

while a throng
of after-tones is spilling
from its iron prison
filling the streets with coppery dreams
and sending birds rising high
on repercussions of shining air
over the unmoved hills

but intoxicating me.
I long for words to break free
of this stale prison
the patrol of its opinions,
long to let loose
such enharmonic sound effects
as these.

On the Day of the Dead
in a high town which roots down
into the depths of the hill
the bell tolls on

and I clobber
an earnest leaden tongue
for words and long
to make them ricochet
through other worlds

to wake up strangers
to widen ripples to the shore
I never reach.

I long for words
to resolve the cadences
of a luminous order,
sound out the listeners
on the Day of the Dead.

In Tempo Rubato

(on retirement an employee might be given a clock)

Sometimes its seconds scoot through the hours
like boys, rudderless and bursting for action,
for news, more news

in a small frantic corner of some cosmos

but only today I saw the sea bathed in its own happiness
and so near I could have . . . but the blue mist of its patience
a Sea of Tranquillity subdued me.

And sometimes it just sits there. Accurate
delegate from a metered life of equal intervals
forgotten at its post

in some monochrome corner of its cosmos.

And I remember when a slight sun was fingering the icing
on the trees, rose infiltrating snow, frost
laying lace on glass

the seconds overflowed and fazed the leaking hours.

I watch the clock's complacent face with pity,
for those who seemed to keep in step with its decisions
were slipping off *in illo tempore,*

defectors from the dreadful march-past of history.

Look, things will bring their own time
like the guests who will bring the wine.
Listen, a long-drawn-out music prevaricates

it is *tempo rubato.*

Beyond the last hairpin I come to a line
of twisted olive trees
they show the devastation of their interminable lives
full-frontally to the road
many of their patriarchal trunks are split four ways from the roots
and hollowed out
by some grief there's no more point in hiding.

All eyes they are, begging by the road.
I eye them too
on days like a beggar, cavernous inside,
on those days a caravanserai of life
seems to have passed on by like a mirage on a wind-plagued
    desert
and there's little, there's nothing to show of it.

But I've seen
these ancients go on fruiting
(if you will call their black and bitter berries fruit).
Today blossoms
in that time before they fruit
the whole grove, young and old alike, from here is mingling
in a single canopy of flowering
the faint green lace trembles under silver leaves
as the wind pours through.
The buds, flowers, fruit spring out of these ancient ruins
year after year.

And seeing that
this morning is a pristine page rinsed clean
of memory and of baggage
another morning for beginning I begin again enrolled in the
    beginner's class
expectant, green
not in-grown thick with roots or certainty
with collections housed in velvet
progeny who return as if I were a Holy mountain.
Today my futures wheel and fan like evening birds.